MW01029508

Little Books of Guidance
Finding answers to life's big questions!

Also in the series:
What Is Christianity? by Rowan Williams
Who Was Jesus? by James D. G. Dunn
Why Go to Church? by C. K. Robertson
What Happens When We Die? by Thomas G. Long
What About Sex? by Tobias Stanislas Haller, BSG

HOW CAN ANYONE READ THE BIBLE?

A Little Book of Guidance

L. WILLIAM COUNTRYMAN

Church Publishing
NEW YORK

Church Publishing
19 East 34th Street
New York, NY 10016
www.churchpublishing.org

Cover design by Jennifer Kopec, 2Pug Design
Typeset by Progressive Publishing Services

Library of Congress Cataloging-in-Publication Data

Names: Countryman, Louis William, 1941- author.
Title: How can anyone read the bible?: A little book of guidance /
L. William Countryman.
Description: New York, NY : Church Publishing, [2017] | Series:
Little boooks of guidance | Includes bibliographical references.
Identifiers: LCCN 2017012379 (print) | LCCN 2017027444 (ebook) |
ISBN 9780898691252 (ebook) | ISBN 9780898692310 (pbk.)
Subjects: LCSH: Bible—Study and teaching. | Bible—Hermeneutics.
Classification: LCC BS600.3 (ebook) | LCC BS600.3 .C68 2017 (print) |
DDC 220.6/1—dc23
LC record available at https://lccn.loc.gov/2017012379

Printed in the United States of America

To all those who have gathered
for scripture study
at Good Shepherd over the years

Contents

How can anyone read the Bible?

This question can be heard in two different ways. It might sound like a cry of exasperation: "I tried it and it's unreadable!" Or it could be heard as a question about whether it's really worthwhile for an ordinary reader to give it a try: "I'm not an expert. How do I hope to make sense of it?"

I understand why some readers give up on the Bible. Parts of it are very readable—in fact, quite gripping. Other parts may seem confusing or boring. Part of the challenge for new readers, then, is figuring out where to begin and how to navigate this vast ocean of words. My goal, in this little book, is to supply some basic guidance to help you along as you start making your way through this great trove of riches—riches that readers have been rediscovering again and again for centuries now.

You may, of course, know some parts of the Bible already. Perhaps you've been hearing passages from it in church for years but without knowing how they fit together in the book itself. Or perhaps you're familiar with some of the most famous texts, such as the

Twenty-Third Psalm or the texts that Handel used in his oratorio *Messiah* or Brahms in his *German Requiem*. Or then again, you may never have had any direct encounter with it at all and are drawn mainly by curiosity.

Either way, the Bible can be confusing because it is not tied together by a single, connected narrative or topic, like most modern books. It's a collection of many different kinds of materials written down over a period of more than a thousand years. Even the youngest parts of it are almost two thousand years old, and the oldest contain stories that go back more than three thousand years.

Still, it does have its own kind of coherence and continuity. Its backbone is a story line unfolding over a very long stretch of time. There are themes that keep reappearing, sometimes in unexpected ways. There are persistent tensions that keep cropping up, just as they do in all of human experience. And what ultimately holds it all together is a sense that every part of it is embedded in God's age-long effort to make Godself known to the minds and hearts of human beings.

My assumption, as I write, is that all sorts of people may pick this book up—some who are curious, some who may be hostile but feel a need to understand what they find objectionable, some who are Christian and want to read the Bible with more understanding, some who are people of other faiths or none, wanting to know more about what lies at the root of Christianity. As to myself, I am a scholar of the Jewish and Christian Scriptures and a Christian for whom the Bible has been a source of new and deeper understanding of my life, the world, and God over many years. And you, the reader, are welcome, whoever you are. I hope you will find something here to help you as you begin or further an acquaintance with the Bible.

So, then, can *anyone read the Bible?*

Yes. For that matter, you can come to know it quite well just by hearing it—like many people over the centuries who could not read or for whom books may have been hard to come by. The writing is not, on the whole, particularly abstract; the vocabulary is fairly straightforward—at least in modern translations. And it provides the immediate rewards of intriguing narrative, beautiful poetry, and spiritual insight—alongside a sense of deep mystery and a numinous quality that tells you there is always more here to explore and understand.

St. Gregory the Great wrote, in the sixth century, that the Bible "has on the surface something to nourish infants and, hidden within, something to hold the minds of the highly educated in awe. It is like a river that is, so to speak, both shallow and deep, in which a lamb may wade and an elephant swim." Even if you are a faltering reader you will find things of great power and wisdom that will capture your attention and become something you want to come back to again and again. For example, take a look at one passage you may already know: Psalm 23, which has sustained millions of people over the ages through times of danger, difficulty, uncertainty, and perplexity:

The Lord is my shepherd, I shall not want.
   He makes me lie down in green pastures;
he leads me beside still waters;
   he restores my soul.
He leads me in right paths
   for his name's sake.

Even though I walk through the darkest valley (*or* the valley of the shadow of death),
   I fear no evil;
for you are with me;
   your rod and your staff—
   they comfort me.

You prepare a table before me
   in the presence of my enemies;
you anoint my head with oil;
   my cup overflows.
Surely goodness and mercy shall follow me
   all the days of my life,

and I shall dwell in the house of the Lord
  my whole life long.

These words speak directly to both the mind and the spirit. Even if some of the images—the shepherd's rod and staff, the anointing of the head—may no longer be part of our everyday experience, they are still simple, direct, and clear. The references to "the darkest valley" (also translated as "the valley of the shadow of death") and to "my enemies" make it clear that this is not just feel-good talk designed to paper over our anxieties. This poem knows that human life can be very hard and can still express confidence that God stands by us. In the end, what the Psalm looks forward to is not just protection from harm but a loving relationship with God.

Like this Psalm, much of the Bible has the ability to speak quite directly to the modern reader. And it typically reveals more of its meaning to us as we read more and discover the depth of its images. You find, for example, that sheep and shepherds keep cropping up in different ways. Kings who rule tyrannically, for example, are described metaphorically as bad shepherds in Ezekiel 34; and Jesus speaks of himself as the Good Shepherd in John 10. At the same time, you see that being an actual shepherd was a low ranking job assigned to youngest sons (like David in 1 Samuel 16)* or to poor hired men (like the shepherds to whom angels proclaimed Jesus' birth in Luke 2). The image of the shepherd turns out to be a complex one: the God who is "my shepherd" in Psalm 23 has volunteered for a job that is both powerful and menial.

The more you read the Scriptures, the more readily you grasp their way of speaking to human life. You begin to see connections you hadn't picked up at first and may discover new dimensions of understanding.

But isn't it rather confusing?

In some ways, yes. People who set out to read the Bible straight through often get bogged down and give it up. One difficulty is that it is made up of so many different kinds of writing: stories, genealogies, ordinances, poetry, proverbs, visionary materials, spiritual advice, parables. . . . And the Bible as a whole isn't organized with an eye to leading the reader along. We've already noted that it's a collection of many different books, and even

---

* How to read references to books of the Bible: a number placed *before* the name is read as "first," "second," or "third" to distinguish books that would otherwise have the same name, as in "First Samuel" here. A number following the book's name designates a chapter in the book (unless, as in a few cases, the book has only one chapter). A number following a colon is a verse number.

some of these individual books were themselves stitched together out of diverse bits and pieces. There can be sudden shifts in topic and tone—and sometimes repetitions of material we've already encountered.

A second difficulty is that these writings are from two to three thousand years old and the world has changed a lot since then. Take government, for example. Institutions that modern readers take for granted—legislatures, independent court systems, elected officials at all levels, law enforcement officers to keep public order, basic notions of human rights—few of these existed in the Biblical period, and even when they did they often functioned in different ways. We use words in modern English to translate ancient terms—"king," for example, to translate Hebrew *melech* or Greek *basileus*—but the ancient role of *king* was far from identical to the modern one. In some ways, then, reading the Bible is like visiting a foreign country with a culture different from our own—one separated from us less by geography than by time.

There are many other areas of cultural difference that you'll encounter. Marriage, for example, was often polygamous in the Old Testament period, and the roles of women differed from modern Western expectations. In fact, they differed from one period to another during the times when the Bible was being written. Slavery was a widespread social institution and changed its

7

character somewhat from one age to another. Differences like these mean that readers are sometimes finding their way through an unfamiliar world.

Political realities also changed repeatedly over the thousand and more years during which the Bible was being written. At times, the ancient Israelites were the dominant power in their region; at other times they were subject to neighboring empires. At times, the early Christians thought they would find a safe place for themselves within ancient Judaism and the Roman Empire; at other times, they despaired of both and began to look instead for direct divine intervention to rescue them from the dangers of their world.

This sounds more daunting than it is. It just means that reading the Bible calls for some alertness as we try to figure out how the context was different from our own. It's helpful to find other people who have been reading longer and can offer counsel. You can find some assistance from books written for this very purpose, a few of which you'll find suggested at the end of this book.

And—GOOD NEWS!—much of the Bible is quite accessible to the modern reader without a great deal of extra information about the history and culture in which it was written. We read Psalm 23, for example, without knowing all about its background and still catch its point quite well.

How do I get started?

The short answer might be, "Pick up a Bible and start reading." But, okay, it may be a little more complicated than that. For one thing, the Old Testament is written in ancient Hebrew plus a few pages in Aramaic, the New Testament in ancient Greek. Even two thousand years ago, Greek-speaking Jews needed translations of the Hebrew Bible, and ever since then most people have been reading the Bible in translations. Even in a single language, modern English, there a great many to choose from.

If you already have a translation at hand, go ahead and give it a try. Often, it will be the one called the "Authorized Version" or "King James Version." It's the most beautiful English translation, and if you're comfortable with its Renaissance English, good for you! It has a drawback, however. The Hebrew and Greek texts that its translators had in the seventeenth century, were not as reliable as those now available; nor did the translators understand the ancient languages as well as scholars do now. For those reasons, a modern translation may serve you better. I recommend the New Revised Standard Version of the Bible (NRSV). It is readily available, based on good modern scholarship, and free of theological partisanship—and in wide use for those very reasons. (It's also the version from which most Biblical quotations in this little book are taken.) For some other good choices see the suggestions at the end of this little book.

Do all Bibles include exactly the same contents?

Actually, no. Different religious traditions may have somewhat different lists of books that they include in the Bible. (The technical term for such a list is a "canon"—from the ancient Greek word for "measuring stick.") In this book, I use the canon accepted by Episcopalians and other Anglicans. You can find it in copies of the Bible where the cover or title page says something like "The Old and New Testaments With the Apocrypha." This canon contains all the Biblical books that are used in the services of the Book of Common Prayer.

The Jewish canon of the Bible contains only the books Anglicans call the "Old Testament." Most Protestants use a canon containing the Old and New Testaments but not containing the Apocrypha. (If this is the canon of the Bible you have, you'll be able to find most of the books mentioned in what follows, but not all.) The Roman Catholic canon places some of the books Anglicans call "Apocrypha" in its Old Testament. The Eastern Orthodox Bible is similar to the Roman Catholic but has additional books. (The most recent editions of the NRSV Bible with Apocrypha include the full Anglican, Roman Catholic, and Orthodox canons.)

If it seems odd that there would be so many different versions of the Bible, the reason lies in the history of books and book-making. Our term "Bible" comes from a Greek word *biblia*, which originally meant simply "books." In the beginning, the Bible was exactly that— a collection of books, not a single volume. Only in the Middle Ages, after paper became available, did it become technically possible to gather all the books together into one conveniently sized volume. For the preceding fifteen hundred years, the Bible was not one book, but multiple volumes with only the canonical lists to tell you exactly what was included. Different groups, separated by language and history, developed slightly different lists.

What should I expect to find?

You can expect to find almost everything you can imagine: history, politics, common-sense advice, poetry, profound wisdom, inspiration, and a sense of what it is to be human that stretches us and demands more of us. And all of it is woven together as the story of God's age-long effort to persuade human beings of God's love and to awaken our love in return.

You will, of course, bring your own expectations to your reading. We all do. But be prepared for the possibility that some of them will be disappointed. The Bible is not all as inspiring as Psalm 23. Nor is it always clear-cut, decisive, and conclusive in its teachings about life, belief, ethics, and other topics of interest to us. Often it makes its point by pressing us to rethink things that we have taken for granted.

Ancient Christians thought of it as a book of mysteries. The surface meaning can be opaque or even offensive. We discover the true meaning only by delving deeper into it through further study, reflection, and, likely as not, through a deepening of our own humanity and growth in the life of the spirit. However much we want a simple, self-evident message that will be immediately clear to everyone, the Bible doesn't often offer it, as the age-long disagreements among its readers show. It is both easier and more truthful to admit that the Bible tells us not so much what our conclusions must be as what things we need to take seriously in trying to form our conclusions.

You will find tensions of many kinds in the pages of scripture—some of which I will highlight in my suggestions about how to read. Often, the Bible's wisdom comes through in the way it hangs on to seemingly contradictory concerns and insists that we need to pay attention to both sides of the tension. You may be surprised, for example, to read "Do not be too righteous, and do not act too wise; why should you destroy yourself? Do not be too wicked, and do not be a fool; why should you die before your time?" (Eccles. 7:16–17) alongside texts saying that God scrupulously rewards the righteous and punishes the wicked (e.g., Ps. 37; Ezek. 18) and yet other texts saying that the righteous may suffer in this life (e.g., Matt. 5:10–11; Heb. 11–12).

The Bible has a tendency to confound our first perceptions of it, but this is not just a game it's playing with us. It is a way to make us dig deeper into what we know and believe about God, the world, and ourselves. It pushes us into further reflection and perhaps even growth in our way of understanding and living in the world.

How do I find my way around this vast amount of material?

There are really two questions here. One is the basic question of how to locate things in the Bible. For ease of navigation, I'm afraid there's no substitute for memorizing the order of the books. But what can be a fairly simple task at age ten or twelve may seem daunting to adults. So at least keep a bookmark of some sort at the list of contents.

It also helps to have a sense of the way related books are grouped together. In the Old Testament you find four basic groupings:

The Torah or Books of Moses (five books)

- Genesis (Creation through Israel's migration to Egypt)
- Exodus (escape from slavery to Mount Sinai and the giving of the Law)
- Leviticus (further laws)
- Numbers (Wanderings in the Wilderness)
- Deuteronomy (a further rendering of the Law at the edge of the Promised Land)

History (twelve books)

- Joshua (occupation of the Promised Land)
- Judges (early history of Israel in Canaan)
- Ruth (story of a Moabite woman who became an ancestor of King David)
- 1 and 2 Samuel (Saul, the first king, and David, who took his place)
- 1 and 2 Kings (from Solomon to the fall of the Israelite kingdoms)
- 1 and 2 Chronicles (a later reworking of topics in the preceding four books)
- Ezra (exile in Mesopotamia and return)
- Nehemiah (rebuilding Jerusalem)
- Esther (the challenges of Jewish life in a gentile empire)

Wisdom and Poetry (five books)

- Job (a vivid treatment of the problem of evil)
- Psalms (the hymn book of the Jerusalem Temple)
- Proverbs (a trove of practical wisdom)
- Ecclesiastes (the Biblical voice of skepticism)
- Song of Solomon (a collection of love poetry)

Prophetic Works (seventeen books)

- Isaiah (prophecies from different periods before and after the Exile)

- Jeremiah (prophecies and narratives about the fall of Jerusalem)
- Lamentations (laments over Jerusalem ascribed to Jeremiah)
- Ezekiel (from a prophet in the Exile)
- Daniel (a late book ascribed to a prophet in the Exile)
- Twelve "minor" (i.e., shorter) prophetic books of Hosea, Joel, Amos, Obadiah, Jonah, Micah, Nahum, Habakkuk, Zephaniah, Haggai, Zechariah, and Malachi, dating to various times from the eighth century BCE onward

In the New Testament:

Narratives about Jesus and his first followers (five books)

- Matthew
- Mark
- Luke
- John
- Acts

Pauline Letters (thirteen books, arranged in order of declining length) Nine letters to congregations:

- Romans (considered Paul's major theological statement)
- 1 and 2 Corinthians (addressed to a fractious congregation)

- Galatians (an angry letter)
- Ephesians (a theological discourse)
- Philippians (a letter to a much-loved congregation)
- Colossians (an unusually "cosmic" theological perspective for Paul)
- 1 and 2 Thessalonians (concerned with the End of the World)

Three letters to pastors:

- 1 and 2 Timothy and Titus (often called the "Pastoral Letters")

One private letter:

- Philemon (concerned with an escaped slave) (It is possible that that some of these letters were written not by Paul himself, but by followers of his, writing in his name.)

Other letters (eight books, arranged in order of declining length)

- Hebrews (more sermon than letter, of unknown authorship)
- James (attributed to the brother of Jesus)
- 1 and 2 Peter (the latter probably the last New Testament book to be written)
- 1, 2, and 3 John (from the same school or author as the Gospel of John)

- Jude (attributed to another brother of Jesus) (As with Paul's letters, actual authorship may be uncertain.)

Apocalyptic (a form of writing with vivid imagery concerned with the end of the world) (one book)

- Revelation of John (not, it seems, by the same person who wrote the Gospel or the three Letters of John)

The order of the books of the Apocrypha is not as standardized as in the Old and New Testaments. The King James Version has the full Anglican canon in the following order, while recent translations may have additional books and different ordering:

- Two books of Esdras, the one narrative, the other an apocalyptic book
- Narratives of life under oppressive imperial regimes: the absorbing stories of Judith and of Tobit and some bits of Esther found in the ancient Greek, but not the Hebrew version of that book
- Two books of wisdom: Wisdom of Solomon (a meditation on divine wisdom in creation and history) and Ecclesiasticus (usually called "Sirach" in modern translations), concerned with issues of behavior and history

- Prophetic writings: the Book of Baruch (Jeremiah's secretary); the Letter of Jeremiah; and three excerpts from the Greek version of Daniel—The Prayer of Azariah and Song of the Three Holy Children; Susanna and the Elders; and Bel and the Dragon
- Two histories of the revival of Jewish independence in the second century BCE: 1 and 2 Maccabees

Okay, so how do I really find my way around this vast amount of material?

Yes, that's the bigger question here: how do I make sense of it all? Begin by reading each book as a work in its own right. Don't worry about how the larger whole hangs together. A few books do form connected sequences, notably 1 Samuel through 2 Kings, which trace the history of the ancient Israelite monarchy, or the books of Luke and Acts, which combine the story of Jesus with an account of important events among his first followers. But most books are complete in themselves.

Second, remember that some books have always been treated as more centrally important than others. For Jewish readers, the Torah (Genesis through Deuteronomy) has always held this place. For most Christians, it is the

Gospels that serve this purpose, though some Protestants, particularly Evangelicals, seem to prefer the Letters of Paul. Some Christians with a particular fascination for the end of the world seem to focus more on Revelation.

Another way to seek a sense of the Bible as a whole is to focus on one *type* of material or another. For example, those looking for clear ethical direction often wind up giving priority to commandments and other legal materials. Others will be more interested in explicit statements of theological ideas. And others may feel that the narrative materials give us the best way to follow and understand the rest.

The Bible itself doesn't tell us which, if any, of these to choose. The choice tends to reflect the interests of the reader. The Torah and the Gospels have the advantage of representing time-tested preferences of whole communities of readers—also true for Paul. Whatever choice is made, we tend to interpret other materials in relation to those considered central.

On the whole, however, newer readers of the Bible will be best served by beginning with the narrative. The story provides a framework in which everything else finds its place. Also, narrative doesn't predetermine interpretation as much as more abstract materials may. Laws and doctrines can even be misunderstood if they are taken out of their historical and cultural context and treated as abstract systems. And efforts to extract a detailed prediction of the End of the World from the Bible have proven conspicuously mistaken. If you can learn your way around the narrative, the rest will come much more easily.

Does it make a difference whether I am a believer or not?

Yes and no. All of us, as readers, bring our preconceptions with us. Some of us take up the Bible expecting to find God speaking through it—whether in so many words or by giving us new understanding and strength for life. Some take it up simply out of curiosity, others because of recognizing that the Bible is a foundational document of Western culture in general. Whatever perspective you bring will shape your reading to a degree, but attentive readers know that good reading means questioning your presuppositions as well as those of the text.

And reading the Bible can work changes in us. Believers may find that their faith changes as they come to know the Bible more deeply. Non-believers may find the world and human life becoming larger, deeper, and more interesting than they had previously supposed. The Bible has a history of prompting its readers to rethink basic assumptions.

Okay, but what is the Bible all about? How about a quick synopsis?

The Bible is the story of God interacting with the world and our human efforts to respond—sometimes positively, sometimes negatively, sometimes wisely, sometimes foolishly, sometimes with understanding, and sometimes quite wrong-headed. In it, God communicates with and through people of all sorts (Job, for example, is an Arab). But God also creates specific bonds with two particular communities—Israel and the church. In both cases, it's a rocky relationship, God's love meeting with faithfulness and betrayal and everything in between. It has all the high drama human life is capable of.

Embedded in this story, poetry gives voice both to the best of our insights and the worst of our misunderstandings. Prophecies focus on how the story centers on God. Wisdom literature tries to knock some basic sense and civility into us. Apocalyptic reveals the depth of our moral quandaries and offers hope for the worst of times.

The implication is always that the story is still ongoing, still being acted out in our own human responses to God—faithful, faithless, generous, stingy, calculating, honest, hopeful, close to despair—with the same tawdriness and grandeur you will find in the stories of our Biblical predecessors and with the same divine desire to bring us into friendship with God.

Reading this book, we may find ourselves by turns elated or horrified, challenged or encouraged—but always beckoned onward by it. It is not primarily a book of answers, but it is an invitation to intimacy with the God whose openness to humankind prompted its writing in the first place.

How will I know whether I'm getting it right?

You won't know whether you are getting it right. After all, as the Gospel of Matthew points out, even the devil can quote scripture (4:1–11). It is a problem with language in general that, try as we may, it is almost impossible to be perfectly clear.

But there are some ways we can, so to speak, check up on ourselves. One way is simply to practice the art of careful reading. Take a second look at the passage. Did we really read it carefully? Read the surrounding passages. Do they suggest something different from our first take on it? Think about how the cultural context of the passage may have been different from ours. Does that change how it might have sounded to its first readers? Think about the Bible as a whole, insofar as you are coming to know it. How does this passage fit in (or conflict) with that?

Ask yourself, too, what you might be ignoring or glossing over, either in the passage you're reading or in other parts of scripture. Some of the great historic wrongs in reading the Scriptures (the justification of the Inquisition, the Crusades, or the Biblical defense of slavery in the nineteenth-century United States) arose when people read passages that appealed to them (about purity of belief, vengeance on enemies, or the ancient law of slavery) and ignored ones that didn't suit their purpose (such as loving one's neighbor as oneself).

Think about what effect your reading of the Bible is having on your own life. Are you becoming more faithful, just, generous, loving, and hopeful—or less? The Bible is written in terms of the world where it was composed—at least as imperfect as our own time. It was written in terms intelligible in its own time. But its point is not to make us go back and imitate the past, but it is to ask how what God was revealing might illuminate our own time and place. Its purpose is to lead us toward growth in spirit.

Pay attention, too, to how other people may read the passage. Sometimes you may have an insight others can benefit from; sometimes others may see what you've missed.

Finally, expect that, as you go on reading Scripture over many years, you will keep finding new understandings even in familiar passages. Our reading is a journey.

Perhaps the main danger is not that you might get something wrong, but that you will become so attached to one particular interpretation that you can't turn loose of it even when your continued reading suggests that you misunderstood. Christians long allowed ancient custom and an obscure curse in Genesis 9 to eclipse the Biblical command to love our neighbors as ourselves in order to support American segregation and South African *apartheid*. Others have used a literalist reading of Genesis 1 to dismiss well-founded insights of modern science. And many still emphasize passages they read as subordinating women to men while ignoring those that speak of the equality of the sexes in Christ (e.g., Gal. 3:28) or of the leadership of women (e.g., Judg. 4). The truth is that, at any given moment, we can grasp only as much as our journey through life and the Bible has prepared us for. Growth in the Spirit and attentiveness both to the text and to the world around us can help us recognize our mistakes.

But what does the Bible offer its readers if it doesn't provide final, precise answers to our questions?

It gives us materials for thinking about the issues as we live with them, and it gives them to us in the form of contradictory ideas that it holds in tension. For example, we are told that God made and loves the whole world and that God chose and loved a particular family of humanity. How does the Bible reconcile the conflicts implicit here? It doesn't. It simply refuses to allow the reader to abandon either side of the quandary.

For example, given that human beings have been in conflict with one another from the beginning, as near as the archaeological record can tell us, how can the God who loves all side with one group against another? One strand in the Bible takes the side of the Chosen against all others. This is the strand that can justify the annihilation of Israel's Canaanite enemies without mercy—or, in the New Testament, can think of God as rejecting Israel in favor of a new chosen group, the church. But alongside this strand is another, pointing out that the Canaanites were not in fact all killed or expelled (one even shows up as late as Matt. 15!) and noting that, awkwardly enough, King David's great grandmother was a Moabite foreigner named Ruth. Again, the Book of Jonah tells a tale about a prophet who would be happy to see the Assyrians, Israel's bloodiest antagonists, doomed to destruction and is furious with God because God is always eager to forgive those who own up to their wrongdoing. God does love Israel—and declines to take on the duty of hating its enemies. God loves the church, too—and declines to reject Israel.

In other words, the Bible doesn't get us out of our awkward quandaries. What it does is to keep us company as we live through them. And it can do this best if we let it proceed in its own way—not by nailing questions shut, but by opening them up and enlarging our perspective.

I don't mean to suggest that there is no focus or direction to be found in the Bible. It is there, but it is a goal toward which we journey. The long tradition of faith suggests that we focus on the overarching, persistent themes that shape the Bible, such as the following:

God is love. God creates out of love. God loves people—and the rest of creation (cf. God's concern for the animals in Jonah 4). God offers friendship to us and asks for our friendship in turn.

As we come to know God's love, it will shape our lives, emerging in love for others and the building of a community in which others, even the poor and the outsiders, are treated with respect.

God insists on justice as the foundation of human community, but is far more eager to forgive and to restore broken relations than to punish.

God's work is an ongoing process. God initiates it, not us; but we are invited to cooperate with it.

God is so committed to the creation and to humanity that God risks living among us—even becoming one of us—in order to make friendship with us a reality. Sometimes this can threaten to taint God with the evils we do in the name of religion, but God still sticks with us because of hope for a future that we can, at this point, only dimly envision—a future in which God's generous and unfailing love will be accepted and shared by all.

Some suggested approaches

Where, then, to begin?

For some people a good answer may be "With the texts that already touch you deeply." There are passages of scripture that keep drawing us back because they have life-changing and life-enhancing potential. Paul's great panegyric on love in 1 Corinthians 13 is an example. The exalted and disturbing creation stories of Genesis 1–3 and the prophecies of hope in Isaiah 52–55 are other examples. The cry of need in Psalm 130 ("Out of the depths I cry to you") or the reassurance of Psalm 23 ("The Lord is my shepherd") are others.

These are always worth returning to because reading the Bible is an ongoing process; it is not something that is taken up, finished with, and put away. With a popular novel, it's enough to be able to say, "Oh, I've read that." With the Bible, a single reading is just the beginning. Each re-reading engages us more deeply and gives rise to reflection on ourselves, our God, our world—not just the texts themselves.

There is no possibility of completely "mastering" the Bible. If we think we know everything it has to say to us, we are just not reading carefully enough—and perhaps not letting it enter into conversation with our own deep hopes and fears, our trust and our longing. It is full of surprises hiding in plain sight.

One weakness, however, of simply returning to our favorite passages is that they don't necessarily lead us to further reading. To get a more comprehensive experience of the Bible, you might want to try a more organized approach. For some, it will be enough to echo Lewis Carroll and say, "Begin at the beginning, then read until you come to the end." I did exactly that with my first Bible, a copy of the Revised Standard Version given to me by my parents when it was first published. Since I was about ten years old and an avid reader, nothing bothered me for long. Even the most boring bits were at least as interesting as the labels on cereal boxes that I read during breakfast. Even long lists of names could be interesting if only because some of them seemed so bizarre. But this is definitely not everybody's way of reading, and even the most dedicated reader will find that there are doldrums to endure and barriers to get over.

In any case, all hardy souls ready to read with abandon are hereby given permission to skip long lists of things like genealogies if they like and to skim repetitious materials. I'll even offer some hints about passages you may prefer to skim:

Exodus 36–39 largely repeats 25–31.

Leviticus 1–7 gives detailed instructions for sacrificial worship that will seem too technical for most readers.

1 and 2 Chronicles largely repeat stories from the preceding four books but sometimes with a quite different twist. Skim them, but keep an eye out for new materials (like Solomon's vision in 2 Chron. 1) or surprising shifts (like Satan's unexpected appearance in 1 Chron. 21 as compared with 2 Sam. 24).

In Jeremiah you'll find some overlap with the end of 2 Kings, but by the time you get there, the refresher course may be welcome.

Ezekiel 40–48 contains a detailed description (with precise measurements) of a visionary rebuilding of Jerusalem.

When you come to the Gospels, read the shortest one, Mark, first. Then, you will more readily recognize the things that are distinctive in Matthew and Luke. John will turn out to be distinctly different from the first three.

Other readers may prefer to follow their own reading preferences. Some of us like stories best because they take us into the nitty-gritty of human life. Some of us like poetry; even those of us who say that we don't often have a favorite poem or two for which we make an exception. Some of us are very interested to see how people think about questions of right and wrong. Some of us are more interested in the broadest possible questions of existence: Who or what is God? What does it mean to be human? Where does evil come from? How do we understand death?

I offer suggestions here for several possible ways to focus your reading. But I do suggest *beginning* with the first of them, because the narratives provide the backbone on which this whole sprawling collection of texts depends. It's easier to grasp the rest of the Bible when you have a sense of the story.

1. Follow the story.

The Bible is full of great stories, from the creation of the world onward. Some of them will inspire you. Some will perplex you. Some will probably (and should probably) shock you. As I said earlier, if you find yourself bogged down by an occasional boring passage, feel free to skip it. The main thing is to keep reading.

From creation to the promised land (Genesis through Deuteronomy): The story begins in Genesis with the creation of the world and humanity and continues with accounts of the first murder, escape from a terrible flood, the wanderings of the patriarchs, and the wisdom and generosity of Joseph, who saves his brothers' lives even after they sold him into slavery. Then, you'll encounter the danger and excitement of the Exodus, as the enslaved Israelites escape from Pharaoh's army, and you'll encounter the boredom, deprivation, and complaints that characterize a long trek through the desert. That's punctuated by the awesome epiphany at Mt. Sinai, but then it's back to the refugee community, missing its familiar context and deeply disoriented—struggling, arguing, and plodding through the desert (though with the wonderful comic interlude of Balaam and his ass in Numbers 22). You'll also find that the narrative is repeatedly interrupted by other materials, particularly legal codes. They, too, have their own interest, but it's all right to skip or skim them while you're tracking the story. You can do that by concentrating on Genesis and the following selections: Exodus 1–20, 24, 32–35, and 40; Numbers 10–14, 16-18, 20–25, 27, 31–32; Deuteronomy 1–4, 29–34.

Israel in a hostile world (Joshua 1-11, Judges, Ruth): There are some grim stories in Joshua and Judges. Some readers may feel a need to move on directly to Ruth, but if you do you won't catch quite how surprising Ruth, with its Moabite heroine, and 1 Samuel, with the beginning of kingship, are.

Rise and fall of Israel as a political power (1 and II Samuel; 1 and 2 Kings): The main focus is on the changing demands of Near Eastern politics, on the challenges of dysfunctional dynasties, on politics and religion, and on the lapses and, occasionally, triumphs of justice. The story concludes with catastrophe—the fall of Jerusalem and exile in Babylon. (1 and 2 Chronicles cover much the same territory but from a somewhat different perspective.)

Exile (Daniel 1–6, Esther, and, in the Apocrypha, the Additions to Daniel and the books of Judith and Tobit): These tales, some famous and some less well-known, take us into the world of Israelites who lived dispersed among the great empires of the ancient Near East—everything from the persecution experienced by minority populations without political power to ways of making a faithful life in exile to heroic resistance on the part of two women, Esther and Judith.

Return (Ezra, Nehemiah): Some of the exiles return to Judah and rebuild Jerusalem. See also the short book of Haggai, written during this time.

A second chance at independence: 1 and 2 Maccabees, in the Apocrypha, tell the story of a successful Jewish revolt against an oppressive Greek empire in the second century BCE.

Jesus and the church (Gospels, Acts, Galatians): Read any or all of the four gospels. Luke might be a good initial choice for following the story, because it leads directly into Acts of the Apostles. Galatians 1–2 will give you a different take on some of the events narrated in Acts, this time from Paul's perspective.

Visions of the End (Daniel 7–12, 2 Esdras, Revelation): These three apocalyptic works offer varying visions, from different eras, of how the story might play out in the future.

This is a lot of reading, you say. *What's most important in all of it?* For Christians, the story of Jesus is the central thing. Begin there, if you like. But the better you know the earlier parts of the story, the better you will understand the gospels. After all, the gospel writers and their first readers all knew and loved these writings. In any case, the earlier narratives are well worth reading in their own right.

2. Go for the poetry.

Poetry can put us in touch with the emotion of situations as well as what people were thinking about them. Here are some suggestions:

Epic (not epic in length, but on the epic themes of history and victory) *includes the following:* The Song of Moses (Exod. 15); the Song of Deborah (Judg. 5); Psalms 18, 105–107, and 135–136. In these you get a sense of the enormous relief from fear that a small, endangered community feels at the destruction of its enemies.

Love songs include the following: Song of Solomon. Yes, erotic poetry right there in the middle of the Bible.

Hymns of praise and trust include the following: Psalms 23, 24, 27, 46, 63, 148, 150; Luke 1:46–55 and 67–79, 2:28–32. These three passages from Luke have entered Christian worship as three of the canticles in Anglican Morning and Evening Prayer—*Benedictus*, *Magnificat*, and *Nunc Dimittis*.

Elegies and songs of grief and distress include the following: 2 Samuel 1 (David's lament over Saul and Jonathan); Psalms 22, 38, 42–43, 69, 130; Lamentations.

Songs of awe and wonder include the following: Psalms 19, 84, 93, 95–96, 131; Philippians 2:5–11; the brief hymns in Revelation 4–5, 7, 11–12, 15, 19, 21.

Songs of comfort and hope include the following: 1 Samuel 2 (Hannah's song); Psalm 23; Isaiah 40:1–11 and chapters 51–55; Wisdom of Solomon 3:1 9; 1 Corinthians 13 (Paul's prose poem on Love).

Poems that challenge God include the following: Psalms 49, 73–74, 77, 80, 88; Ecclesiastes.

Poems that meditate on the meaning of life include the following: Job (a long argument about the problem of evil and justice with an astonishing conclusion); Psalms 1, 139; Ecclesiastes; Wisdom of Solomon 11–8.

3. Seek out advice for daily living:

There is a trove of sound advice in Proverbs and in Sirach in the Apocrypha (called "Ecclesiasticus" in older translations but not to be confused with Ecclesiastes in the Old Testament). The advice is addressed to young men in a very different era, but it is astonishing how on-target much of it still is in our world. Some of it is purely practical. Some emphasizes the values of integrity and generosity that lie at the heart of all civility and morality.

Jesus takes up this tradition and sometimes turns it on its head, as in the Sermon on the Mount, which generations of readers have found both inspiring and challenging (Matt. 5–7). Luke 6 is similar. Some of Jesus' parables present a similar kind of wisdom, particularly the parables of the Good Samaritan (Luke 10:23–37) and the Rich Fool (Luke 12:13–21).

The early followers of Jesus also had quite a lot to say about standards of behavior, particularly where they confronted problems in congregations. Many New Testament letters conclude with a bit of general advice about behavior: for example, Philippians 4:8–20; Colossians 3:1–4:5; 1 Thessalonians 5:12–22; and Hebrews 13. Romans 12–15 is devoted almost entirely to questions of how Christians of very different backgrounds can live together within the church community, as is much of 1 Corinthians. The wonderfully down-to-earth Letter of James often sounds very much like the earlier tradition of Hebrew wisdom found in Proverbs and Sirach.

4. Look for spiritual understanding:

Psalms are texts that were sung in worship at the ancient Temple of Jerusalem and have continued to be used by Jews and Christians alike as one of our basic forms of prayer. Morning and Evening Prayer in the Anglican tradition are built around the recitation or singing of the Psalms. These poems reflect a vast array of human emotions: fear, anger, hope, distress, adoration, uncertainty, trust. . . . On first reading, many of them may seem foreign to any given reader—if only because you don't share the state of mind and spirit that they reflect. Still, you will probably recognize those emotions from other times in your own life. Some Psalms express vengeful sentiments that other parts of the Bible teach us to forego; but even if you find them objectionable now, you will recognize their authentic human feeling. In effect, the Psalms bring everything human into the relationship with God. No aspect of us gets left out. And that turns out to be one of the basic building blocks of the spiritual life. As Psalm 139 says, there is no point in trying to hide your real self from God; it won't work anyway.

Song of Songs is a book of erotic poetry that may not seem, at first glance, like a place to look for spiritual understanding. But that's exactly where both Jewish and Christian readers have turned for centuries. The songs of the two human lovers here have given many religious people the best language we have for the love between human beings and God. St. John of the Cross and Henry Vaughan, for example, followed in this tradition.

Isaiah is a long book with many different kinds of materials in it. In fact, it was probably composed over a period of several centuries—by the original Isaiah and at least two successors. Some things to look for: Isaiah's own account of his prophetic calling, his emphasis on social justice as integral to true religion, the hope of restoration after disaster (beginning particularly in chapter 48) and the meditations on the meaning of suffering often called the "Servant Songs" (42:1–9; 49:1–6; 50:4–9 and 10–11; 52:13–53:12).

In Jeremiah, we have the great interpreter of the decline and fall of the Kingdom of Judea. In a dangerous time, his message was unpopular and his life often endangered (chs. 1, 7–9, 15–20, 26–29, 32–44). Jeremiah tells us a great deal about his prophetic calling and challenges God in his prayers for having laid this burden on him.

Jonah is a rather funny story that reminds us that our piety can come between us and God. Jonah's hatred of evil keeps him from understanding or sharing God's love and compassion.

Matthew has the great Sermon on the Mount (chs. 5–7) that has been inspiring and intimidating people for close to two thousand years, as it describes a kind of life that we recognize as both truly humane and also seemingly beyond us. The Parables of the Kingdom (chs. 13; 20:1–16; 22:1–14; 25) speak of the power of God to change the world, the unexpected ways in which God does so, and the challenge this poses for us. The story of Jesus' suffering, death, and resurrection (chs. 26–28) serves, in effect, as the ultimate parable of how God approaches humanity and invites our response.

John is a Gospel that is focused on God's incarnation in our world in the person of Jesus, who reveals God's intention through signs and words. It also speaks of how the believer becomes one with him and, through him, with the One who sent him (17). It is a founding document of Christian mysticism.

Romans 1–11 is Paul's great summation of how our relationship with God arises out of God's graciousness rather than our own achievements of piety. This doesn't make human goodness irrelevant, but focuses spirituality on the generosity of God instead of the isolated, striving self.

1 Corinthians 13 speaks of love as the one central and enduring element in human life.

Philippians finds the pattern for human spirituality in Jesus' self-emptying in order to become one of us (2:1–11).

1 John focuses on the declaration that "God is love" and keeps drawing everything back to the centrality of love for human existence.

5. Seek the roots of law and justice.

The Torah or Law of Moses is one of the foundations of the Western understanding of justice. But it belongs to a very different era from ours, and the modern reader can be perplexed at the way in which profound ethical concerns are mixed together with directives concerned rather with issues of physical purity, worship, and ethnic identity. A few selections, for the sake of focus: Exodus 20, 23; Leviticus 19 (notice in both Exodus and Leviticus how profound ethical concerns are mixed with ceremonial ones); Deuteronomy 5–7 (here ethics of universal significance stand alongside things we would now reject, such the prohibition against showing mercy to defeated enemies in 7:1–6). This underlines what we said earlier about God's revelation being given to people in their own particular times and places and in forms that they can understand and embrace. There are thus elements in the Scriptures that we have to reject in our times—with the understanding that our own perspective may be historically limited, probably in ways we cannot fully recognize.

The Psalms repeatedly stress devotion both to the Torah and to the ideal of justice in particular. Psalm 119 is a long hymn in celebration of the law, and Psalms 72, 99, and 146 speak of the importance of justice to the work of the king and the life of the nation.

Proverbs 10–15 stresses the importance of justice alongside other basics of civility, good judgement, and responsibility—things as useful and valuable for our times as for the ancient audience.

One of the great themes of the prophets was the centrality of justice and its importance to the survival and well-being of the nation. See, for example, Amos; Isaiah 1 and 58; and Micah 6.

Jesus' Sermon on the Mount (Matt. 5–7) is allusive and elusive and resists yielding any clear-cut theory of justice. From one perspective, Jesus appears to be making the provisions of the Torah more demanding—close at times to impossible. Adultery and murder, after all, are avoidable, but what about "looking with desire" and being "angry with a brother"? Another way to look at this is that Jesus is shifting the focus, both ethically and spiritually, away from specific prohibitions and toward an acknowledgement of our human finitude and an ideal of loving even those who do not love us (5:43–48).

The Letter of James harks back to the tradition of Proverbs, uniting ethics with other kinds of wise advice, but here, too, the emphasis seems to rest on an honest understanding of our own limitations and James's vision of how God has made the last first and the first last within the new community of the church (1:9–11; 2:1–13).

6. Celebrate creation.

The two different creation stories in Genesis 1 and 2 reach their climax, in a sense, with the creation of humanity, but this does not mean that they exalt humanity as something over against nature. The Adam of Genesis 2 is a gardener, not a despoiler of nature; and if God says to the new humans of Genesis 1, "Have dominion," that simply describes the kind of dominance humanity has long demonstrated in practice. One could think, in Genesis 2, of the garden as God's main interest, with Adam merely a helper. And, in the first creation story, the true climax is not the creation of humanity, but the Sabbath (Gen. 2:1–3) on which God rests and delights in the created world.

Biblical poets knew how to embrace this kind of delight, as in Elihu's speech (Job 37) and God's response to Job out of the whirlwind, ranging from the original creation to the wonders of the animal world (Job 38–41).

In the Psalms, we find a celebration of the heavenly bodies (19), a vivid evocation of storm (29), a comprehensive sense of the world of animals (including human beings) (104), and a carefully observed panorama of weather (147).

Isaiah makes songs about creation and new creation (11:1–10; 25:6–9; 40:1–31; 65:17–25).

In the Apocrypha, the Additions to Daniel include the Prayer of Azariah and the Song of the Three Jews— exuberant celebrations of the created order that have provided two canticles for Anglican Morning Prayer— *Benedictus es* and *Benedicite*).

Revelation 21:1–22:7 places a great park with a river running through it in the heart of the new creation.

7. Search for God.

The Bible is not as simple and direct on this subject as we sometimes assume. The Biblical writings were distinctive in speaking of God as *one* in a world where most people assumed there are many gods, often working at cross purposes to each other. But while the Biblical authors teach that there is only one true God, they sometimes acknowledge that there are other, lesser powers at work in the world. Psalm 82 tells a story about the one God deposing all other gods because they committed injustice. And Paul (1 Cor. 8:4–6) also acknowledges that the world is full of gods, even while insisting that only one God really counts. Gods that were worshipped in the form of images came in for particular scorn (Isa. 44:9–20; Jer. 10).

The one God is the creator, as in Genesis 1 or Amos 5:8–9. And this can raise questions about the goodness of God, given the imperfections of this world. Isaiah 45:5–7 states the problem in the plainest of terms. Ecclesiastes acknowledges that much in this world seems accidental or unjust and warns against expecting perfect justice in this life. Job's long argument with God about justice ends in a moment of awe and acceptance—not an explanation. John's Gospel represents God as voluntarily suffering the injustice of human life alongside us.

At the same time, there is a strong emphasis on God's concern for justice in contrast both to the moral indifference of some other gods and to our widespread human tendency to place our own interests and convenience ahead of justice for our neighbor. It is a point made in many places, among them the book of Amos, Isaiah 5, 1 Kings 21, and Psalms 72, 99, 103, and 146. In the New Testament, James, and I John say emphatically that injustice to the weak cuts us off from God—a point found in Jesus' teaching, too.

God is also seen as the source of all wisdom, which is even personified and identified with God in Proverbs 8–9, in Sirach/Ecclesiasticus 24, and in Wisdom of Solomon 6–11. In the New Testament, Wisdom reappears as Logos, a Greek term meaning "word," "speech," or "reason." And in the *Logos*, according to John 1, God becomes incarnate in Jesus.

God is identified explicitly with love in 1 John. But even before that identification is made, God is repeatedly described as loving, merciful, and forgiving—a theme at least as important in speaking about God as the theme of justice.

8. Contemplate death.

As with the subject of God, the Bible doesn't offer a single understanding of death, but it offers a range of ideas and images. Death is introduced in Genesis 3 as a consequence of the sin of the first humans, but not much is made of that idea afterward until Paul (Rom. 1–8). Sirach/Ecclesiasticus treats death as simply an aspect of the nature of human beings (41:1–4).

Death was often thought of as transporting human beings to a shadowy existence in Sheol, as seen in the story of the medium at Endor (1 Sam. 28). But this kind of "life after death" was not something desirable because it cut people off not only from their families but even from God (Pss. 88, 115, and 143). This is not very distant from thinking of death as a simple extinction of human life, which seems to be the view of Ecclesiastes.

Death, when it followed on a long, full life seems not to have been thought a great evil (Gen. 25:8). It became an evil when it was premature and violent, as in the case of Job's children (Job 1) or when it fell on an entire city or nation through conquest, as seen in prophetic oracles of woe and in the Book of Lamentations.

The idea of an immortal spirit that is not really harmed by death appears in Wisdom of Solomon 3. Another development in thinking about life after death was the idea of a resurrection of the whole person rather than the survival of the disembodied spirit. This thought may lie behind the conclusion of Psalm 17. It became widespread in first-century Judaism and is found throughout the New Testament. Indeed, the resurrection of Jesus is seen as inaugurating a new and more intimate relationship between God and humanity.

The idea of a general resurrection became part of Christian expectations about the End of the World, as in 1 Thessalonians 4:13–5:11 and in the Revelation of John. Subsequent Christian spirituality has sometimes merged the ideas of immortality and resurrection. But the Bible, taken as a whole, contains a much broader range of thinking on this subject.

A reminder.

There is much more to the Bible than I have suggested above. Even these brief guides to particular topics are just starting points. The more extensively you read, the more you will find to add to them. My goal here has been simply to help readers get started by pointing you toward some passages that are likely to capture your interest and provide you an initial base from which you can broaden your reading.

What does it all mean?

The psalmist writes:

> How deep I find your thoughts, O God!
> > how great is the sum of them!
>
> If I were to count them, they would be more in num-
> > ber than the sand;
> >
> > > to count them all, my life span would need to be
> > > like yours.
> > >
> > > (Ps. 139:16–17, 1979 Episcopal Book of Common
> > > Prayer)

There can never be any neat summary of what the
Bible means. Efforts to do that wind up having to
suppress or ignore much that is important in the Bible
in order to come up with a tidy result. The earliest
Christians had a better idea. They went to the Bible
(or rather to their multiple volumes of scripture), looking not for a systematic exposition but rather for a
conversation in which God would speak to them in
the context of their own lives and times. They found
many kinds of meanings in it—some of them seemingly

contradictory. But they were prepared for this by their understanding that the Bible, like the God of whom it speaks, is a mystery—a profound mystery that reveals itself only bit by bit. Indeed, this is the way we begin to understand the profound mystery of our own lives.

Christians have long called the Bible "the Word of God." But we mean this only in a kind of secondary sense. The true Word of God, in the fullest sense of the term, is not the Bible, but God's own self, incarnate in Jesus of Nazareth (John 1:1–18). A person, it seems, can reveal God in a way no book can achieve. The Bible, for Christians, is not an end in itself. It points toward Jesus, whether implicitly in the more ancient writings or explicitly in the New Testament.

The Word of God, then, is not primarily about ideas. Sometimes, Christians have assumed that understanding the Bible is essentially an intellectual endeavor. The process certainly does include the intellect, but it is much more than that. It is an endeavor that has to engage the whole self—a spiritual and existential endeavor. And like any endeavor that involves the whole self, it is a risky undertaking. You will find yourself comforted and assured of God's love in the Bible—and also challenged and judged and even perhaps turned inside out at times. You will also find what the Epistle to Hebrews calls "a great cloud of witnesses" (12:1)—other people who have encountered God and left behind some record.

But I don't wish to conclude with too solemn an impression. The stories and poems and meditations that make up the Bible haven't lived on for two and three thousand years solely because they are profound. They have lived because they are fascinating, intriguing, exciting, and revelatory. That is enough to start with. The rest will make itself known.

True understanding grows with time. It grows as we ourselves grow in it. But we will never come to a point where the mystery disappears. In truth, it cannot. The mystery is something and someone we can encounter in awe and love—and not something we can reduce to propositions or claim as a possession.

Suggestions about books

Translations of the Bible:

The New Revised Standard Version of the Bible (NRSV) is the best English translation over all. Its predecessor, the Revised Standard Version (RSV) is still quite usable, too.

For those who prefer a translation in a more specifically British form of English, the Revised English Bible (REB) is a good choice.

The Jerusalem Bible (JB) is a very good modern translation made by Roman Catholic scholars.

The Good News Translation, also called The Today's English Version (TEV) may be more accessible for people who have learned English as a second language.

The Common English Bible (CEB) is a new and lively translation by a worldwide team of experts in the Bible and in translation.

Basic Commentaries:

The New Oxford Annotated Bible (Oxford University Press, several editions from 1973 and later) contains the full text of the Bible with brief but helpful introductions and comments.

Two one-volume Bible commentaries that offer more detail are:

HarperCollins Bible Commentary, James L. Mays, ed. (HarperCollins, 2000)

The New Jerome Biblical Commentary, Raymond E. Brown et al., eds. (Prentice Hall, 1990)

Broad context:
John Riches, *The Bible: A Very Short Introduction* (Oxford University Press, 2000) gives an excellent survey of how the Bible came into being and how it has been received and read over the centuries.